JORVIK

POMPEII AND
HERCULANEUM

TROY

SITE OF
MESOPOTAMIAN,
ASSYRIAN AND
SUMERIAN CITIES

KNOSSOS

PERSEPOLIS

MOHENJO-DARO
INDUS VALLEY

TIMBUKTU

ANGKOR

GREAT
ZIMBABWE

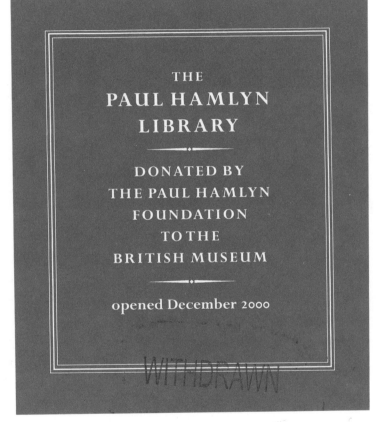

TREASURE HUNTERS

THE SEARCH FOR

LOST CITIES

NICOLA BARBER

MACDONALD YOUNG BOOKS

This book is dedicated to Peter Barber

First published in Great Britain in 1997 by Macdonald Young Books
an imprint of Wayland Publishers Limited

Find Macdonald on the internet at http://www.wayland.co.uk

© Macdonald Young Books 1997

Macdonald Young Books
61 Western Road
Hove
East Sussex
BN3 1JD

Concept Designer: Jane Hannath
Designer and Typesetter: Kudos
Illustrator: Mark Stacey, David Lewis Agency
Map Illustrator: Bruce Hogarth, David Lewis Agency
Map Calligraphy: Oriol Bath, David Lewis Agency
Commissioning Editor: Fiona Courtenay-Thompson
Project Editor: Caroline Arthur
Assistant Editor: Lisa Edwards
Series Editor: Nicola Barber

Photograph Acknowledgements: AKG photo p.11(tr), 19(ct) 19(bl), 20(tr), 25(bl), 29(tr),
31(tl), James Davis p.42(bl); e.t.archive p.37(tr); Mary Evans p.12(bl), 17(cr), 28(cr),
33(tl), 35(br), 37(br); Robert Harding p.15(tl), 15(tr), 38(cb), 39(br); Peter Hicks
p.24(bl), 25(tr); Michael Holford p.12(ct); Hutchison p.39(tr); Photri p.41(tr), 41(bl);
South American Pictures p.31(cr); Tony Stone Worldwide p.26(ct); Topham p.9(tr);
Eye Ubiquitous p.8 (bl), 34(cb); Wayland p.43(br)

Picture Researcher: Shelley Noronha

Printed in Hong Kong by Wing King Tong

A CIP catalogue record for this book
is available from the British Library

ISBN: 0 7500 1912 3

Cover artwork: Colin Sullivan

CONTENTS

INTRODUCTION

'**I**t fairly took my breath away. What could this place be? Why had no one given us any idea of it?' These are the words of the explorer Hiram Bingham, written after his astonishing discovery of the spectacular ruined Inca city of Machu Picchu. (See page 33 for more about Bingham's search.) Machu Picchu had lain forgotten for over 300 years. Other cities have been 'lost' for many hundreds, and even thousands, of years. But how do cities get lost? And how do people set about finding them again?

The ruins of the Inca city Machu Picchu lie high in the Andes Mountains in Peru.

HOW DO CITIES GET LOST?

It's hard to imagine today's modern cities being abandoned and becoming 'lost'. How could anyone forget a city as large and as famous as London, or Paris, or New York? The answer, of course, is that cities don't usually just disappear overnight. Often, they decline over many years, until the last people leave their homes and the buildings fall into ruins. Some abandoned cities are gradually covered by dust and mud until they are nothing but shapeless mounds. Some are swallowed by jungle, and their once grand buildings are smothered and hidden by plants. Others are pulled down as people remove building materials to construct their own new settlements nearby. Gradually, people forget that there was ever a bustling city in their area, and as the memory fades the city is 'lost'.

Archaeologists can piece together the history of a city from tiny clues.

How does a city die?

There are many possible reasons for the death of a city. For example, some cities grew up beside busy trading routes. But sometimes trade decreased, and then the city declined too. In other places, changes in the climate affected the life of cities. Perhaps the land around a city became less fertile, so there was not enough food to feed all its inhabitants, and gradually people had to move away.

The end of other cities was more sudden and spectacular. Natural disasters such as earthquakes and volcanic eruptions wiped out places such as Pompeii (see page 22). Sometimes, fires burned down whole cities. And sometimes, cities were destroyed on purpose. The magnificent city of Persepolis, the capital of the Persian Empire in the sixth century BC, was burned down by the army of Alexander the Great in 330 BC.

The ruins of the ancient city of Persepolis are in modern-day Iran.

Alexander the Great orders his soldiers to destroy the Persian city of Persepolis.

Finding lost cities

Although cities may be abandoned for many years, they are not usually truly lost. Often, the local people will know of hidden ruins or mysterious buried walls. It is only when an outsider comes looking for evidence of a forgotten city that anyone realizes what the ruins really are. This was true of Hiram Bingham, who was led to the Inca ruins of Machu Picchu by a local man who knew exactly where they were. In other places, archaeologists have painstakingly put together evidence to work out what a city was once like. We begin our search for lost cities with a look at some of the earliest cities and some of the people who discovered what we know about these cities today.

THE EARLIEST CITIES

The ancient region of Mesopotamia lay between the Tigris and Euphrates rivers. Today this region is part of Iraq.

For hundreds of years, people in Europe have known about and admired the remains of the fine buildings of Ancient Greece and Rome. After the invasion of Egypt in 1798 by the French general Napoleon Bonaparte, news of the great pyramids and temples of the Ancient Egyptians also reached Europe. People thought that these spectacular ruins were the remains of the oldest civilizations in the world. But in the nineteenth and twentieth centuries, in Mesopotamia and further east in the Indus Valley, new discoveries were made: the remains of developed and well-organized civilizations which were far, far older. This is the story of these discoveries.

BIBLICAL CITIES

The land of Mesopotamia lies in modern-day Iraq, between the great Tigris and Euphrates rivers. In fact, the name Mesopotamia means 'land between two rivers'. It was in this area that the world's oldest cities flourished. Many of these cities are mentioned in written records such as the Bible, from which we know about Nineveh, Jericho, Babylon and many others. But compared to the beautiful ruins of Ancient Greece, Rome and Egypt, the remains of the ancient towns and cities of Mesopotamia were not exciting to look at. These once great cities were dismissed as hardly better than mounds of mud – until people started to take an interest in them in the early nineteenth century.

Claudius Rich

The first that most Europeans heard about the Biblical cities of Mesopotamia was a report about a mound known as Hillah, not far from Baghdad. This mound, and others near it, covered the ruins of the ancient city of Babylon. The mound was first explored in 1811 by a British official, Claudius Rich.

Claudius Rich had a great talent for languages, and by his teens he knew Latin, Greek, Arabic and many others. After several years of travelling, he was given an important job in Baghdad, and he went to live there with his young wife, Mary.

Rich was fascinated by the archaeological riches of the region, and he began to collect ancient objects and manuscripts. In 1811, he managed to arrange a trip to look at the ruins of Babylon. He spent two weeks measuring and sketching, and in 1815 he published a book about his discoveries. It was an instant success, and Europeans became very curious about the cities of Mesopotamia. In particular, people wanted to know more about the cities mentioned in the Bible. Were they real places? If so, did they still exist – even as ruins?

Excavating Babylon

It wasn't until the end of the nineteenth century that any major excavations were made at the site of Babylon. A German archaeologist called Dr Robert Koldewey directed the dig, which lasted seventeen years. Dr Koldewey uncovered the remains of massive city walls with watchtowers. These huge walls were wide enough for a four-horse chariot to be driven along the top, and they measured 17 kilometres round, making Babylon the largest city in ancient Mesopotamia. The archaeologists also found the ruins of a stepped temple known as a ziggurat, which was originally about 91 metres high. This temple probably inspired the story of the Tower of Babel in the Bible.

The magnificent Ishtar Gate formed the main entrance to the city of Babylon.

A relief carving in stone from one of the palaces in Nineveh. The scene shows an Assyrian king, Ashurbanipal, at a feast with his queen in their royal garden.

REDISCOVERING THE ASSYRIANS

The first people who tried to find out more about Rich's discoveries in Mesopotamia were the French. In 1840, the French government sent a historian called Paul Emile Botta to the city of Mosul in northern Mesopotamia. Botta began to dig at a mound which we now know was the site of ancient Nineveh. But he was disappointed with what he found at Nineveh – a few bricks stamped with ancient writing and some broken pieces of sculpture. One day, a local man told Botta that his village, at some distance from Nineveh, was built on a mound of sculpted stones and more inscribed bricks. In fact,

the local people used the ancient bricks to build their own houses! Botta decided to investigate. Everything was just as the man had said, and Botta uncovered the city of Khorsabad, the ancient capital of the Assyrians and home of the great King Sargon II (ruled 721–705 BC).

Eastern enthusiasm

Meanwhile, a British man named Austen Henry Layard was also keen to investigate the ancient mounds of northern Mesopotamia. Layard was so enthusiastic about the East that he had given up training as a lawyer in order to go there. His travels were full of adventure – Layard was often robbed, and frequently turned up at the end of a journey half naked and stripped of all his possessions! But he wasn't discouraged. He met Botta while the Frenchman was working at Nineveh, and luckily the two men got on very well.

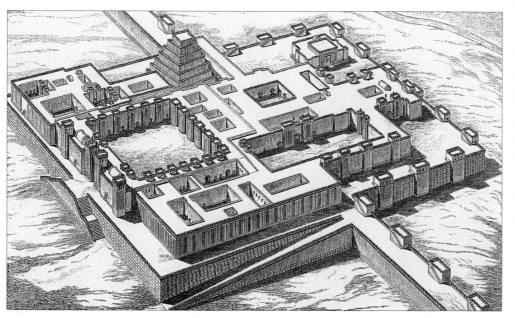

A reconstruction of King Sargon's palace in Khorsabad

Layard decided to excavate a mound at Nimrud. Over the next few years, he uncovered magnificent palaces with brightly coloured wall-paintings and elaborate sculptures. The entrances to these palaces were guarded by gigantic figures of winged bulls and lions. With great difficulty, Layard managed to remove one bull and one lion and take them back home to England. When they were shown to the public in Britain, Layard's Assyrian sculptures caused a sensation. Today, his collection is kept in the British Museum in London. Botta also shipped home hundreds of Assyrian artefacts, many of which are in the Louvre Museum in Paris.

Who were the Assyrians?

The Assyrian Empire covered much of the north-west of modern Iraq. The first empire was conquered by the Babylonians in 1760 BC. But 1,000 years later, the Assyrian kings Tiglath-pileser III and Sargon II built up another enormously powerful empire. Sargon built a new capital and magnificent palace at Khorsabad. The palace had sculptures of battle scenes and strange bull-men along the walls. However, the city of Khorsabad was abandoned when Sargon died. The whole Assyrian Empire crumbled only 100 years later, in the early seventh century BC, after repeated rebellions and attacks.

Layard oversees the removal of one of the great winged bulls from the city of Nimrud.

13

Back in time

For most of the nineteenth century, people thought that the newly discovered empires of the Babylonians and the Assyrians were the world's earliest civilizations. But in the 1870s, archaeologists started to find evidence of an even older civilization, based in southern Mesopotamia. The people of this civilization became known as the Sumerians. However, nobody knew much about the Sumerians until the 1920s, when Sir Leonard Woolley started to excavate the city of Ur.

Woolley dug down through layer after layer at Ur, gradually finding evidence of older and older settlements. The bottom layer showed that the earliest people lived there about 7,000 years ago. These people were the very first farmers. Woolley found stone hoes for turning the soil and clay sickles for cutting crops, as well as cow dung mixed with mud to make walls, and a small model of a pig. Woolley's slow and careful excavations revealed thousands of years of Sumerian life. About 5,500 years ago, the Sumerians were building grand ziggurats (temples) to their gods, and 4,500 years ago they buried their dead kings and queens in elaborate royal tombs, surrounded by rich treasures.

AN UNEXPECTED DISCOVERY

In 1857, a British engineer called John Brunton arrived in Karachi in modern-day Pakistan. His job was to supervise the building of a new railway across the valley of the River Indus, north of Karachi. Before leaving the city, Brunton heard tales of an old city somewhere near the route of the railway. He decided to look for the city, in the hope of finding materials, such as bricks, that he could use to build foundations for the railway tracks. So he set off with several camels and a local guide, and two days later reached the mysterious city.

Brunton was amazed at the size of the city. He spent some time exploring it and writing a description of the walls around it and its 'royal palace'. He also found some coins and some seals

with pictures and symbols on them, which he took away with him. Then he returned to Karachi, and gave orders for many of the ancient bricks to be removed to build the railway!

A forgotten civilization

The city discovered by John Brunton is known as Mohenjo-daro. It had been almost totally forgotten for about 4,000 years when Brunton set eyes on it. In fact, it was forgotten once again after Brunton's visit. Nobody took much notice of the British engineer's descriptions of this city built of bricks. But how did it come to be there, and why had it been forgotten for so long?

Today we know that Mohenjo-daro was one of the many cities, towns and villages of the Indus Valley civilization, which flourished between about 5,000 and 4,000 years ago. What is strange is that all these settlements seem to have vanished completely by about 1750 BC. There is nothing about the Indus Valley civilization in any written records. Yet this civilization covered a larger area than either Mesopotamia or Ancient Egypt.

The cities of Mohenjo-daro and Harappa lie in the valley of the Indus River in modern-day Pakistan.

The ruins of Mohenjo-daro, showing clearly the sun-baked bricks with which the city was built

The earliest town planning

When excavations did begin at Mohenjo-daro in the 1920s, the archaeologists in charge of the dig were amazed by the layout of the city. The streets of both Mohenjo-daro and another Indus Valley city, Harappa, 560 kilometres to the north, are laid out on a grid. The roads cross at right-angles, dividing the city into blocks, like the street plan of New York. Obviously, these cities had been carefully planned. What's more, both cities had complicated drainage systems. Houses had baths and toilets, and there were drains to take away the dirty water.

In some areas of Mohenjo-daro, there were small workshops where specialist craftspeople made pottery, cloth, jewellery and other items. Scholars think that the Indus Valley people may have traded with the Mesopotamians to the west. The huge numbers of seals that have been found in the Indus Valley cities certainly seem to be evidence of a great deal of trade (see box).

The end of Mohenjo-daro

What happened to bring such an advanced and well-organized civilization to an end? No one knows for certain. It seems likely that the Indus Valley cities began to decline, then were attacked by invaders and easily defeated. Archaeologists have found many skeletons marked by sword cuts in the most recent remains of Mohenjo-daro. Clearly, people were struck down and murdered with little mercy. Is this a vital clue to what brought about the end of the Indus Valley civilization?

UNREADABLE SEALS

John Brunton took away with him several seals from Mohenjo-daro. Since then, hundreds more of these seals have been found in the Indus Valley. They were used by merchants who traded goods such as pottery, timber and ivory. Many of the seals are marked with a kind of picture writing. Altogether, there are nearly 400 different symbols. However, so far no one has managed to decipher this 4,000-year-old writing.

Seals from Mohenjo-daro marked with animals and a kind of picture writing

SEEKING ANCIENT GREECE

Ancient Greece, showing the sites of some of the most famous ancient cities

'**I am among the ruins of Homeric Troy!**' the German archaeologist Heinrich Schliemann wrote in his diary on 18 June 1872. Schliemann was writing about his excavations at a remote spot known as Hisarlik in western Turkey. Here, Schliemann claimed to have found the remains of the famous city described in the *Iliad*, an epic poem by the Ancient Greek writer Homer. But had Schliemann really discovered Homer's Troy? Some people were not so sure.

AN EXTRAORDINARY LIFE

Heinrich Schliemann always said that he had been fascinated by Homer and his stories of the Trojan War from a young age. In his autobiography, he wrote that even as a boy he was determined to find the true site of the lost city of Troy. In fact, there is no real evidence that Schliemann was particularly interested in Troy until much later in his life. As we shall see, Schliemann's stories about his childhood are just one of many doubtful claims he made about his life.

What is certainly true, however, is that Schliemann was an extraordinary man. He travelled all over the world, making huge fortunes during the gold rush in California and through business deals in Russia, France and elsewhere. He trained his memory so strictly that he could learn a foreign language completely in a matter of weeks, and using this method he mastered fifteen different languages. At the age of forty-one, he decided to retire from business and to spend his money on archaeology, particularly on finding the mysterious city of Troy.

First, though, Schliemann wanted a wife! He had recently divorced his first wife, and in 1869 he wrote to a Greek friend asking for help in finding a second wife. He was very particular about what he wanted: 'She must be poor, but well educated; she must be enthusiastic about Homer . . . she should be of the Greek type, with black hair, and, if possible, beautiful.' Amazingly, a suitable girl was found. Her name was called Sophia Engastromenos, and the two were married in the same year.

Digging up Troy

Before starting to dig at Hisarlik, which he was convinced was the site of ancient Troy, Schliemann had to get permission from the Turkish government. This was not as simple as he had first hoped, and it was more than two years before he was given a permit. When Schliemann finally set off to Hisarlik in October 1871, his permit allowed him to dig on three conditions: that he must share any finds half-and-half with a Turkish museum; that he must leave the ruins in the same state as he found them; and that he must pay all the expenses of the dig. As we shall see, Schliemann took very little notice of the first two of these conditions!

Over the following two years, Schliemann returned to the ruins of Hisarlik many times, with huge teams of workers. His loyal wife, Sophia, often went with him too. But as the excavation went on, Schliemann began to realize that there wasn't just one Troy on the site – there were many different Troys! As his workers dug huge trenches through the ruins, they came across layer after layer of remains. Several different cities had been built one on top of the other over the centuries. Which one of these cities was the Troy that Homer had described, where Hector and Achilles had battled so fiercely?

HOMER AND THE *ILIAD*

Homer was a Greek poet who lived at some time in the eighth century BC. His epic poem, the Iliad, *is based on the story of a ten-year war between the Trojans and the Greeks. The war starts when the Greek king's wife, Helen, is stolen away by Paris, son of the Trojan king, Priam. Furious, the Greeks attack the city of Troy. After ten years of terrible war, during which heroes such as Hector and Achilles, and Paris himself, are killed, the Trojans are eventually defeated, and the Greeks take their revenge.*

Heinrich Schliemann

Schliemann and Sophia watch the excavations at Hisarlik.

Which Troy?

From the evidence of the ruins, Schliemann decided that Homer's Troy would be one of the bottom layers. Homer's heroes fought with weapons made from bronze, so Schliemann was looking for a layer dating from the Bronze Age. In his determination to go straight down to the lowest level, he ordered his workers to dig deep trenches and move huge amounts of stone and rubble. He didn't examine the higher levels of the ruins very closely. But in 1873 he realized that he had dug too deep. The city ruins he had uncovered were too old to be Homer's Troy. Unfortunately, the excavations had destroyed a large area of the city that Schliemann now thought was the one he was looking for. Many people were not sure that this second city was the right one, either. However, an amazing discovery convinced Schliemann that he was right.

'Priam's treasure'

Early in the morning of 31 May 1873, Schliemann was working in the ruins near an area which he had called the Palace of King Priam, after the Trojan king in Homer's poem. Suddenly, he caught sight of a large copper object – and, beyond it, the glint of gold. Schliemann later wrote that as soon as he saw the gold he ordered his workers to take a rest. Then he dug out the treasure and handed it to Sophia, who hid it in her shawl. There was a copper shield, a silver vase and a copper plate, and then more cups and plates. Even better, inside the silver vase were golden earrings, bracelets and rings.

Schliemann smuggled the treasure out of Turkey, avoiding having to hand over half of it to the Turkish museum. The treasure was hidden in Greece. When Schliemann published his book about the excavations at Hisarlik, the Turkish government was furious. But none of the treasure ever went back to Turkey. What's more, Schliemann later admitted that Sophia hadn't been with him when he found 'Priam's treasure' – she was far away in Athens.

According to his account, Schliemann handed 'Priam's treasure' to his wife, Sophia, as he dug it out. Later, this story was found to be untrue.

18

Return to Troy

Schliemann went on to excavate at Mycenae, in Greece, where he claimed to have found the death mask of Agamemnon, the king who had led the Greeks into battle in the *Iliad*. Despite his arguments with the Turkish government, he even returned to Hisarlik for more excavations. Schliemann also visited Knossos, on the island of Crete, and announced that he was going to dig at this interesting-looking site. But this never happened. He died in 1890, and the story of Knossos belongs to another man: Sir Arthur Evans.

Sophia Schliemann wearing the magnificent jewellery that formed part of 'Priam's treasure'

Gold hairpins from the treasure

THE FATE OF THE TREASURE

What happened to 'Priam's treasure'? Schliemann gave the treasure to a museum in Berlin, Germany. During the Second World War, the treasure disappeared. Some people thought that the precious gold jewellery had been melted down. Others said that the treasure went to Russia, where it was hidden deep in a vault in a Moscow museum – and, luckily, they were right! In April 1996, Priam's treasure went on display for the first time in fifty years, in a museum in Moscow.

A gold drinking vessel, beaker and bottle, all found by Schliemann at Hisarlik

'Priam's treasure' as first displayed by Schliemann at his house in Athens

DISCOVERING THE MINOANS

Sir Arthur Evans must be one of the few people in the world who have made an exciting discovery as a result of being extremely short-sighted! His sight was so bad that, without glasses, everything around him was a blur. However, he could see tiny details on small objects held a few centimetres from his eyes. One day, he picked up some small seals and gemstones in an antiques market in Athens. It was only because of his short sight that he noticed the tiny markings on their sides. He was told that the seals and gemstones came from Crete. The next year, he went to the island for the first time. After visiting the site of Knossos, his mind was made up – he would excavate there.

Sir Arthur Evans in his study in 1925, surrounded by artefacts from his excavations at Knossos

Evans began work at Knossos in 1900. It was soon clear that he would find far more than the seals and clay tablets he was looking for. One of the first things that his workers uncovered was the remains of a great palace! He had discovered evidence of a civilization that had been forgotten for over 3,000 years. Evans decided to name this civilization 'Minoan', after Minos, who, according to Greek legend, was once King of Crete.

THE FORGOTTEN EXCAVATOR

Sir Arthur Evans is the man who is always given the credit for rediscovering the forgotten Minoan civilization, but he was not the first person to excavate at Knossos. In 1878, a Cretan man called Minos Kalokairinos began to dig some trenches at the site. He found pottery and other objects, and realized that the area should be properly excavated. But when he applied for permission, he was turned down by the government. At that time, Crete was ruled by Turkey, and the Cretan government was afraid that any treasures found at Knossos would be taken to museums in Turkey. So Kalokairinos was forgotten, and the world remembers only Sir Arthur Evans for his work at Knossos.

The palace at Knossos

The palace that Evans uncovered had over 1,500 rooms and a complicated layout of corridors and courtyards. Evans identified the throne room, and found the rooms where the royal family had lived in some comfort. There were also many store rooms, and workshops where potters, jewellers, carpenters and stonemasons worked. Evans rebuilt walls and staircases, and put new roofs across some of the rooms. He also hired painters to complete the wall-paintings around the fragments he had found. You can still see Sir Arthur Evans' reconstruction of the palace at Knossos today.

The walls of the rooms in the palace of Knossos were covered in brightly coloured wall-paintings.

The end of Knossos

What happened to bring the flourishing Minoan civilization to an end? Like Schliemann at Hisarlik, Evans found that there were different layers of ruins at Knossos. Around 2000 BC, the Minoans built several palaces, one after another, but they were all destroyed by earthquakes. Then, some time around 1500 BC, the volcano on the island of Santorini (sometimes known as Thera) to the north of Crete erupted. The eruption was huge and violent. Was it this that destroyed Knossos and wiped out the Minoan civilization? (See page 42 for more about the end of the Minoans.)

MINOS AND THE MINOTAUR

According to Greek legend, a hideous monster, half bull and half man, lived on the island of Crete. This monster, called the Minotaur, inhabited a huge underground maze known as the Labyrinth. Every year, King Minos of Crete fed the Minotaur with human victims from Athens. But the Minotaur met its match when the son of the King of Athens, Theseus, came to Crete. With some help from Minos's daughter, Ariadne, Theseus killed the Minotaur and escaped from the Labyrinth.

Could this story be based on truth? Many people have noticed the maze-like design of the palace at Knossos. What's more, bulls were obviously an important part of Minoan life. One of the most famous of the Knossos wall-paintings shows acrobatic bull-leapers seizing the bull's horns and flipping neatly over its back.

FROZEN IN TIME

The morning of 24 August AD 79 was quiet and rather hot. The people of Pompeii, in southern Italy, were uneasy. There had been small earthquakes for several days now, shaking the ground and damaging some buildings. Some of the freshwater springs in the city had suddenly stopped flowing. But no one was prepared for what came next.

VESUVIUS ERUPTS

A few kilometres to the north-west of Pompeii lay the volcano Vesuvius. It had not been active for over 1,000 years, and its fertile slopes were covered with vineyards and small fields. But on that fateful morning, Vesuvius suddenly erupted, with a massive explosion that sent red-hot lava thousands of metres up into the air. A cloud of black dust and ash blotted out the sun, and tonnes of ash and lava rained down on the surrounding countryside. There were violent storms, with blinding flashes of lightning, and more explosions from the volcano as it belched out poisonous gases into the air.

The people of Pompeii heard the first tremendous explosion. But there was little time for escape. As the hail of hot ashes and lava fell on the town, some people ran into their houses for cover. Others ran towards the sea, trying desperately to escape from the town. Soon, walls and ceilings began to collapse under the weight of the lava, and people suffocated in the fumes and the dust. In the pitch dark, it was impossible to see where to go, and many people were trampled to death in the panic. About 2,000 people died in and around Pompeii.

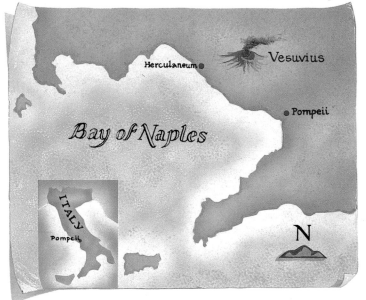

Vesuvius lies on the Bay of Naples, in the south-west of Italy.

In the neighbouring town of Herculaneum, too, the inhabitants were amazed by the first massive explosion. But the cloud of dust and ash did not blow their way. Instead, a huge river of mud and lava flowed slowly towards the town. As the mud covered Herculaneum, it destroyed everything in its path. But it moved slowly enough to allow most people to escape. Only twenty or thirty people were killed.

We know a lot about the terrible fate of Pompeii from two letters that the Roman writer Pliny the Younger wrote in AD 104 to the historian Tacitus. Pliny was staying with his mother at nearby Misenum when Vesuvius erupted. This is how he described the horror of that day: 'And now came the ashes, not yet falling very thickly. I looked round. A dense black cloud was coming up behind us, spreading over the earth like a flood. "Let's go into the fields while we can still see," I said, "or we shall be trampled underfoot by the people on the road." We had scarcely done this when darkness fell . . . You could hear the shrieks of women, the wailing of children and the shouting of men . . . At last, the darkness thinned . . . and the sun shone, but yellowish as in an eclipse. We were terrified to see everything changed, buried deep in ashes like snowdrifts . . .'

Forgotten cities

Pompeii was left covered in a layer of lava up to 5 metres deep. Herculaneum was drowned under a sea of mud between 15 and 18 metres deep. Where the towns had stood there was nothing but an empty landscape of black, smoking lava. As the years passed, grass and trees began to grow in the volcanic soil, and the area became fertile farmland. The region was known as La Civita ('The City'), but this was the only reminder of the cities that were now buried deep underground. Even the name Pompeii was forgotten.

Panic sweeps through the town of Pompeii as ash and lava rain down from the erupting Vesuvius.

Over 1,500 years later . . .

In 1594, a nobleman living in La Civita gave orders for a tunnel to be built to carry water from a nearby river to his villa. As the workers dug the tunnel out, they were amazed to come across parts of ancient buildings and pieces of brightly coloured wall-paintings. But neither they or the nobleman took much notice of the discovery.

Over 100 years later, in 1709, a local farmer was digging a well when he struck a layer of white marble. An Austrian general heard about his find and immediately bought all the land in the area. He wanted the rich marble for building material. His team of workers made deep excavations and found beautiful statues and marble columns, which they took away to put in the general's country house.

In the 1730s, the Queen of Naples saw the beautiful objects in the general's villa and gardens and was captivated by them.

A wall-painting from a house in Pompeii

She begged her husband to look for more treasures. The king put another general, Rocco Gioacchino de Alcubierre, in charge of new excavations. He dug tunnels at both Herculaneum and Pompeii, and in 1763 he found a stone bearing the inscription RESPUBLICAE POMPEIANORUM ('the commonwealth of Pompeii'). At last the name of Pompeii had risen from the ashes.

The ruins of Pompeii as they look today

POMPEIIAN FASHIONS

During the eighteenth century, people all round Europe were fascinated by the story of Pompeii. Buildings and furniture were designed in the 'neo-classical' style; ladies wore dresses copied from Pompeiian wall-paintings and china manufacturers such as Josiah Wedgwood based their designs on pots found at Pompeii.

The 'Homer' vase by Wedgwood

24

Treasure seekers

The aim of these early excavations at Pompeii and Herculaneum was to find and remove any valuable objects. Alcubierre and the excavators who followed him were quite happy to strip the wall-paintings and sculptures from the buildings that they uncovered, and they were particularly keen to find as many precious objects, such as jewellery, as possible. A few people protested at this plunder, but it was 1860 before the scholar Giuseppe Fiorelli started proper, careful excavations in Pompeii.

Fiorelli divided the city into nine areas, and worked methodically on one area at a time. As far as possible, he left wall-paintings and statues where they were, and he made careful notes of exactly where things were found. In some places, Fiorelli covered the exposed ruins with new roofs to protect delicate paintings and objects from the weather.

Fiorelli's scientific methods were later copied by archaeologists in Pompeii and Herculaneum. Today, you can walk around the remains of both cities.

Cities frozen in time

What makes these cities special is that they weren't special! Neither Pompeii nor Herculaneum was the centre of a great civilization, or the home of a powerful king. They were ordinary cities of their time, lived in by ordinary people. When Vesuvius erupted, people were busy doing everyday tasks such as baking bread or spinning wool. Both Pompeii and Herculaneum are full of evidence of how ordinary people lived in the first century AD. The cities were frozen in time by their terrible fate, but this is what makes them so fascinating to us today.

A loaf of bread from ancient Pompeii. The bread was in a bakery oven when Vesuvius erupted. The volcanic ash sealed the oven and preserved the bread intact.

Swallowed by Jungle

The main temple in Angkor, called Angkor Wat

'There are few sensations sadder than seeing lost and deserted cities which were once scenes of glory and pleasure.' These are the words of a French missionary, written in 1850 after his visit to the ruined city of Angkor, deep in the jungles of Cambodia. The missionary was impressed by the size of the huge buildings, which were all overgrown with creepers and other plants. But what was this city that lay crumbling and in ruins deep in the jungles of South-east Asia? The missionary was not to know that he had stumbled across what was once one of the largest cities in the world.

KAMBUJA

The city of Angkor was built by the people of the Khmer Empire between 1,000 and 550 years ago. The city was started by King Jayavarman II, who freed the Khmer people from the rule of the Javanese and declared independence for the country of 'Kambuja'. The modern-day name Cambodia (or Kampuchea) comes from this ancient name.

Jayavarman chose the site for his new capital carefully. The city was at the centre of his new kingdom. It stood beside the Tonle Sap, a huge lake whose waters flowed (via two other rivers) into the important Mekong River, making travel and communication easy. There was plenty of wood for building in the forests that covered the region. But what made the site so special was the Great Lake itself.

Angkor was built near the Tonle Sap, or Great Lake. The ruins of Angkor lie in modern-day Cambodia.

A city built on religion

Most of the buildings of Angkor were made of wood, and so they have not survived to tell us how the ordinary people of the city lived. Nor do we know what the royal palaces were like, because they were also built from wood. What have survived, however, are the spectacular ruins of gigantic stone temples. These temples are so large and so splendid that Angkor was obviously a major religious centre.

The religion of the Khmer people originally came from India and was distantly related to Hinduism. The Khmer kings were worshipped by their subjects as gods. Each king built a temple during his own lifetime which, after his death, became his tomb. The most famous of all these temples is Angkor Wat, built for King Suryavarman II, who ruled over the Khmer Empire from AD 1113 to 1150.

A city built on waterways

Every spring, as the snows melted in the Himalaya Mountains to the north, the water was carried away by rivers flowing down from the mountains. The Mekong River became so full that the water flowed up the connecting rivers into the Great Lake, making the lake grow to three times its normal size. When the flooding went down, the overflow from the lake drained back into the river again. But while the lake was flooded, millions of fish came to feed off the underwater vegetation. This provided plenty of food for the Khmer people. What's more, the flooding fertilized the soil around the lake, making it possible to grow good crops of rice. The people of Angkor relied on the waters of the Great Lake in order to survive.

Jayavarman ordered huge building works, starting with waterways called *barays*. Vast numbers of slaves built high embankments. Some of these protected buildings from flooding. Others were built close together to form deep channels, which filled up with rain and river water in the wet season. In the dry season, this water was used to irrigate the fields. For hundreds of years, the people of Angkor continued to build elaborate systems of canals and reservoirs.

A CHINESE VIEW

We know very little about the lives of the ordinary people of Angkor. But one eye-witness account of life in the city was written by a Chinese official called Chou Ta-kuan, who visited it in 1296. He described the appearance of the king: 'The king usually wears a crown of gold . . . Around his neck he wears about three pounds of large pearls and around his wrists and ankles, and on his fingers, bracelets and rings of gold set with cats'-eyes [precious stones].' But Chou Ta-kuan also noticed the poor living conditions of the ordinary people, especially the slaves, who were treated cruelly.

The king, as he appears on a temple in Angkor

Angkor Wat

Angkor Wat was probably the biggest religious building ever built in the world. It was surrounded by a moat 180 metres wide, with a bridge leading to the main gateway. Its central tower was over 60 metres high, and the five main towers were decorated with more than 10,000 elaborately carved stone pinnacles. Every square centimetre of this huge building was covered in fine carving, including one scene which was over a kilometre and a half long. Thousands of slaves, craftspeople, stonemasons and sculptors must have been needed to construct such a massive building.

Only half a century after Angkor Wat was completed, the last king of the Khmer, Jayavarman VII, carried out a building project that was even more ambitious than Angkor Wat. He rebuilt the capital city, giving it the name Angkor Thom ('The Great Capital'). This new city was surrounded by thick stone walls, and at its centre was Jayavarman's temple, the Bayon. The Bayon is covered with about 200 huge faces, each about 2.5 metres high. Jayavarman also gave orders for hundreds of hospitals and other buildings to be constructed all across the empire.

The end of the Khmer

Some people think that Jayavarman's extravagant building projects helped to bring about the end of the Khmer Empire. They say that all this building cost far too much and exhausted the Khmer people. Other people think that something went wrong with the irrigation system, or that the soil became less fertile. Whatever the reason, the Khmer Empire was taken over by the neighbouring Thai people. In 1432, Angkor was attacked for the last time and finally abandoned by its inhabitants. Quite rapidly, jungle plants smothered the buildings, and the great city of Angkor was completely forgotten.

A drawing made in 1895 of one of the terraces in Angkor Thom. The relief sculptures show an elephant procession.

SHIVA WORSHIP

Many of the kings of Angkor worshipped the Hindu god Shiva. In fact, the kings saw themselves as Shiva's representatives on earth. According to Hindu tradition, Shiva is the god of both destruction and creation, and he lives with the other gods on the top of Mount Meru. The temples built by the Khmer kings symbolized Mount Meru, the home of the gods. The Khmer believed that building these huge temples and carrying out the correct religious ceremonies were the only things that would make the rice crops continue to grow and the irrigation system continue to work. Otherwise, the empire would collapse.

The Bayon temple is covered with huge stone faces.

EERIE FACES

Even as Angkor re-emerged from the jungle, it lost none of its mystery, as the words of one French archaeologist show. Here he is describing his feelings as he suddenly notices the massive faces of the Bayon temple: 'I looked up at the tree-covered towers . . . when all of a sudden my blood curdled as I saw an enormous smile looking down at me, and then another smile over on another wall, then three, then five, then ten, appearing in every direction. I was being observed from all sides . . .'

French explorers

The French missionary who glimpsed the ruins of Angkor in 1850 was the first European to visit the region. But the person who is usually said to have 'discovered' Angkor is another Frenchman, Henri Mouhot. Of course, the local people in Cambodia knew about the mysterious lost city in the jungle, but no one had thought the ruins were specially remarkable, as the jungles of Cambodia were full of the remains of ancient temples. The local villagers told Mouhot that Angkor was 'the work of giants'. Mouhot, however, was very excited by what he found, and set about measuring and sketching the crumbling buildings.

Mouhot's book about his travels in Cambodia sparked off huge interest in France and elsewhere. How old was the city? And who had built it? Unfortunately, Mouhot never knew about the success of his book, because he died of a fever on the way home from Angkor.

Faces appear through the tangle of jungle.

But as a result of Mouhot's enthusiasm, French archaeologists travelled to Cambodia and worked at Angkor for many years. They cleared away the creepers and trees that had smothered the ruins and brought the city of Angkor out into the light once more.

LOST IN AMERICA

When a sailor on board Christopher Columbus's ship sighted land in 1492, he was possibly the first European ever to set eyes on the 'New World'. At that time, there were three flourishing and powerful civilizations in the Americas. This is the story of the search for the lost cities of two of those peoples: the Maya of Central America and the Incas in South America.

CITIES OF THE MAYA

In 1517, three Spanish ships were caught in a storm in the Caribbean Sea. When the wind and the waves died down, the crews found themselves near a strange coast. In the distance they could see buildings, palaces and large pyramid-shaped stone temples. These Spanish sailors were possibly the first Europeans to catch a glimpse of the splendours of the Maya civilization.

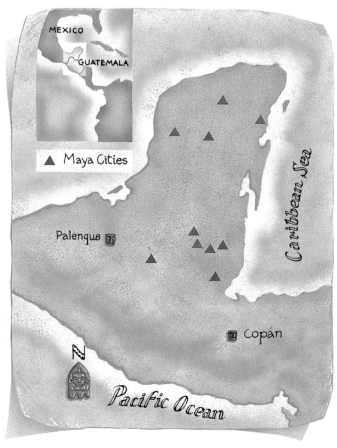

What happened next is well known. The Spanish *conquistador* (conqueror) Hernán Cortés landed in Mexico with a small army in 1519. Over the next few years he conquered both the Aztec and the Maya peoples. The splendid cities of these great civilizations were abandoned as the local people were forced to work for the new Spanish settlers. Missionaries arrived to convert the local people to Christianity, and the local traditions and religions were quickly replaced and forgotten.

Strange reports

The ruins of the Maya cities were forgotten for over 200 years. Then, in the late 1700s, the Spanish authorities heard strange reports of ruins deep in the jungles of Central America. They sent an army captain called Antonio del Rio to investigate. He spent months cutting a path through the thick jungle undergrowth, until he came upon the remains of several stone buildings. This was the Maya city of Palenque. Del Rio wrote a book about his adventures, and other expeditions followed in his footsteps, finding more ruins deep in the jungle.

Despite these investigations, most people did not know about the Maya ruins or the Maya people until an American lawyer came on the scene in 1839. John Lloyd Stephens was not the first person to visit the Maya cities of Palenque and Copán, but he is usually described as the discoverer of these 'lost' cities because he told the public of Europe and America about them.

John Lloyd Stephens

John Lloyd Stephens was a keen traveller. When he was twenty-nine years old, he gave up his job as a lawyer and set out to travel through Europe and the Middle East. He was the first American to reach the city of Petra in Jordan. On his way home, he met an

A painting by Frederick Catherwood of a Mayan temple

The ruins of Palenque in Mexico as they are today

architect and artist called Frederick Catherwood, who shared his love of travelling. The two men became great friends.

Stephens wrote two best-selling books about his journeys. When he decided to set off for the jungles of Central America, he had no trouble raising money for the expedition. What's more, he persuaded his friend Frederick Catherwood to come with him. Catherwood's job was to make drawings of any ruins they found.

Stephens buys a city

Stephens and Catherwood decided to make for Copán, one of the cities described by earlier explorers. They had many adventures on their way to the city. The paths were knee-deep in mud, and once they were arrested! When the two men eventually arrived in the small village of Copán, there was one last problem. The local man who owned the land where the city stood was not very keen to let the two travellers explore the ruins. In the end, Stephens persuaded the landowner to sell him the land, city and all! Stephens paid fifty dollars for Copán.

STUMBLING THROUGH THE JUNGLE

This is how Stephens described the excitement of discovering the ruins of Copán deep in the jungle, in his book Incidents of Travel in Central America: 'It is impossible to describe the interest with which I explored these ruins. The ground was entirely new; there were no guide-books or guides . . . We could not see ten yards before us, and never knew what we should stumble on next. At one time we stopped to cut away branches and vines which concealed the face of a monument, and then to dig around and bring to light a fragment, a sculptured corner of which protruded from the earth. I leaned over with breathless anxiety while . . . an eye, an ear, a foot, or a hand was disentombed . . .'

Sketching Copán

Catherwood set to work to draw the ruins of Copán. It was not easy. The ruins were covered with jungle plants, so the two men hired some local workers to help them clear the stonework. Catherwood had to wear gloves to protect his hands and arms from mosquitoes, his paper was damp, and he seemed always to have a fever. Added to all this, the site was very wet and muddy. These were hardly ideal conditions. Yet Catherwood's drawings were both accurate and very beautiful. When Stephens eventually published his book about the journey, *Incidents of Travel in Central America*, he used Catherwood's drawings to illustrate his story. As before, the book was a best-seller, and it sparked off great interest in the Maya and their lost civilization.

Catherwood endured miserable conditions as he drew and painted in the Central American jungle.

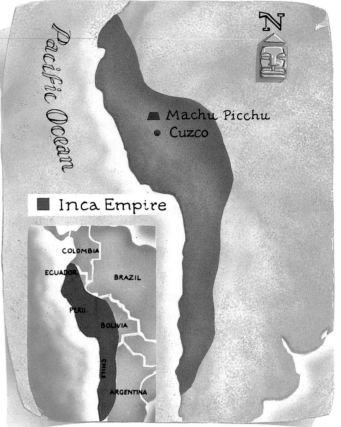

The extent of the Inca Empire

LOST CITIES OF THE INCAS

In 1532, a small band of Spanish *conquistadors* landed on the coast of the Inca Empire. The Incas had ruled over this huge empire, which stretched more than 3,200 kilometres down the western coast of South America, for over 100 years. Yet these Spanish *conquistadors*, led by Francisco Pizarro, took control in only a few weeks!

The Spanish were lucky. Only a few years before, a terrible disease had swept through the empire, killing thousands of people – including the Sapa Inca (Inca emperor). Then there was a terrible civil war over who should become the next Sapa Inca. When the Spanish landed, this civil war was just coming to an end. But the empire was divided and weak, and the Spanish easily captured the new Sapa Inca and murdered him.

In 1533, Pizarro conquered the Inca capital, Cuzco. He also chose a young Inca nobleman, Manco, to be the new Inca emperor, under strict Spanish control.

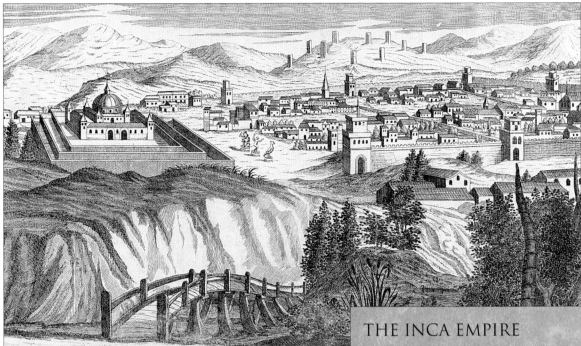

An engraving made in 1760 showing Cuzco, the capital of the Incas

Manco soon realized that he had no real power, and he organized a rebellion against the Spanish. As before, the Inca forces were defeated, and Manco had to escape into the mountains. According to historical documents, he set up his own capital at a place called Vilcabamba, and used a nearby fortress town, Vitcos, as a base from which to attack the Spanish invaders.

THE INCA EMPIRE

The original Incas were members of one tribe, which was based near Cuzco. In the early 1400s, they began to conquer other local tribes. They soon controlled a huge area of western South America, including parts of modern-day Peru, Ecuador, Colombia, Bolivia and Chile. The Incas managed to rule their enormous empire by having a very strong army, and by building a road network to connect every part of the empire to the capital, Cuzco. This is where the Inca emperor, the Sapa Inca, lived, and it was the centre of Inca government.

Enter Hiram Bingham

Nearly 400 years later, a very tired explorer scrambled after his guide – a local farmer – up a steep mountainside. Their route that day had already taken them over a fast-flowing river on a rickety bridge made from a few logs tied together with rope. The explorer, Hiram Bingham, had crawled along the bridge on his hands and knees, but his guide had simply taken off his shoes for better balance and walked over. After several hours of steep climbing they came to a clearing, and Bingham finally glimpsed what he had come for – ruins.

Everywhere there were fine stone walls and staircases, covered in undergrowth. Bingham took some photographs of the walls and also of the amazing views, for the ruins were perched on the side of a mountain, surrounded by other, even higher, peaks. In his notebook he wrote down the local name for the mountain, 'Machu Picchu'. Then he went back to his base camp, ready to move on the next day.

Hiram Bingham

33

The search for Vilcabamba and Vitcos

The discovery of Machu Picchu took place on 24 July 1911. Hiram Bingham was an American historian who was also an intrepid explorer. He had made his first expedition to South America in 1909, and was so enthusiastic that he raised enough money to return there in 1911. The aim of the second expedition was to find Inca ruins, in particular the 'lost' cities of Vitcos and Vilcabamba, from where the Incas had fought their final battles against the Spanish invaders.

So what were the ruins that Bingham had seen that July day? In August 1911, Bingham found some more Inca ruins, which fitted in perfectly with the historical descriptions of Vitcos. He began to wonder whether the ruins at Machu Picchu were, in fact, what was left of Vilcabamba, the last capital city of the Incas. In 1912, he went back to try to find out.

Uncovering Machu Picchu

The first task was to remove all the plants that had grown over the ruined city. Forty local people were paid to climb up to the mountain ridge and work on the ruins. As the massive walls were gradually uncovered, Bingham photographed them. He also photographed graves where the workers dug up the skeletons of the people who lived in Machu Picchu. No gold or silver treasure was found on the site, but there were a few bronze objects, lots of pieces of pottery and some stone dishes. The position of all these finds was carefully recorded.

However, it was the stone ruins themselves that were the most magnificent. There were temples and palaces, as well as smaller houses. On the west side of the city was a sacred stone dedicated to the Inca sun god, Inti. It seems that this was part of an observatory, from where priests noted the passing of the seasons and observed the stars.

The ruins of Machu Picchu lie high on a mountain ridge.

34

HOW WAS MACHU PICCHU BUILT?

How did the Inca builders manage to construct this stone city? Machu Picchu is at a height of 2,300 metres, on a rocky outcrop surrounded by steep drops on all sides. The stone was taken from the mountain itself, and it is hard granite. Some of the stones in the walls weigh many tonnes. The Incas had not invented the wheel, so they must have had large gangs of workers to drag the stones into position. The walls are very well built, with each stone carefully shaped to fit snugly with its neighbours. How the Inca stonemasons cut the stones so skilfully without iron tools is another question that has not yet been answered.

The riddle solved?

Hiram Bingham later wrote many books about his travels in South America, and his 'discovery' of Machu Picchu in particular. He always said that this city was Vilcabamba, the last capital of the Incas. But more recent explorations elsewhere have uncovered what are probably, in fact, the ruins of Vilcabamba. Most historians now think that Machu Picchu was a royal estate, belonging to one of the Inca emperors. What we do not know, however, is what happened to turn Machu Picchu into an abandoned ruin. Maybe an epidemic killed off all its inhabitants? Or maybe it was captured by a rival tribe? It seems likely that Machu Picchu was deserted before the Spanish invasion in the 1530s, but we shall probably never know the complete answer to this part of the riddle.

Special clerks, called *quipucamayocs*, were trained in the use of the *quipu*.

KEEPING RECORDS

The Incas divided their huge empire into four provinces. Every year, each province had to pay a tax in the form of food to the central Inca government. The food was used to feed the nobles and priests, soldiers in the army, and the old and the sick. It was vital to keep track of who had paid what. To do this, the Incas used quipus. *A* quipu *was a long cord with lengths of knotted woollen thread hanging from it. The knots, the colour and the length of the cord were all used to record information.*

35

STRANGE TALES

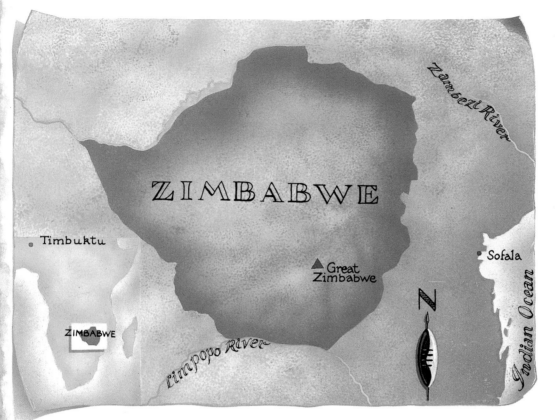

The ruins of Great Zimbabwe lie in present-day Zimbabwe.

I n an area of south-eastern Africa between the Zambezi River and the Limpopo River, there are thousands of ruined stone buildings. About 480 kilometres south of the Zambezi and 400 kilometres inland from the Indian Ocean are the grandest and most impressive of all these ruins, known as Great Zimbabwe. Ever since a European traveller first laid eyes on the ruins of Great Zimbabwe in the 1860s, people have argued about what the buildings were once used for. Even before the nineteenth century, strange tales were told about this 'square fortress . . . built of stones of marvellous size . . .'

AN UNKNOWN LAND

For centuries, Africa was an unknown land to Europeans. After much of northern Africa was conquered by Muslim Arabs in the seventh and eighth centuries AD, links between Europe and most of the African continent were broken. There was still trade between Africa and Europe (for example, much of the gold for European coins came from the goldfields of western Africa), but it was strictly controlled by the Muslim rulers. No Europeans were allowed to travel into the African interior, beyond the coast. Some Arab writers wrote about their travels in Africa, and of the great trading centres such as Timbuktu, Jenne and Gao, but few people in Europe could read Arabic. As a result, Africa became a land of great mystery for most Europeans.

In the early 1400s, Portuguese ships began to explore south around the coast of West Africa. Each expedition took the Portuguese a little further, until, in 1487, Bartholomew Dias sailed round the southernmost tip of Africa. In 1498, another Portuguese explorer, Vasco da Gama, reached India. The Portuguese set up trading posts along the African coast, protected by forts with soldiers. One of these trading posts was at Sofala on the east coast of Africa. From here, Portuguese merchants brought home exotic stories about King Solomon's mines and the Queen of Sheba.

TIMBUKTU, THE FORBIDDEN CITY

In the 1400s and 1500s, Timbuktu was an important city for both trade and learning. Its fame spread far and wide, reaching the ears of many people in Europe. But the Muslim rulers of northern Africa did not allow Christians across their lands, and the city remained forbidden to curious Europeans. That is, until a Frenchman called René Caillié decided to travel to Timbuktu. He disguised himself as a Muslim traveller and, in 1828, succeeded in entering the 'forbidden city'. He was rather disappointed! The days of Timbuktu's glory were long past, and many of the stories about the city had been hugely exaggerated. All he found was a city of 'ill-looking houses built of mud', with no streets or pavements lined with gold. By way of consolation, however, Caillié returned home safely and was given a 10,000-franc prize for being the first European to reach Timbuktu and survive!

A drawing of Timbuktu dating from the 1830s

King Solomon's mines

In the Old Testament of the Bible, King Solomon was said to have built a fleet of ships which went on trading voyages to the land of Ophir. The ships returned carrying cargoes of gold and silver, precious gemstones and sandalwood, and exotic animals such as apes and peacocks. According to the stories told by the Portuguese merchants, and by Arab historians before them, the region around Sofala was the fabled land of Ophir – where Solomon obtained his golden wealth.

The story was made even more thrilling when another Portuguese merchant said that some great stone ruins inland from Sofala were once storehouses belonging to the amazingly wealthy Queen of Sheba. According to the Bible, the Queen of Sheba visited Solomon in Jerusalem, arriving with a great camel caravan bearing precious stones, spices and huge amounts of gold. From the merchant's description of the ruins of the 'storehouses', it is possible he was talking about Great Zimbabwe.

Solomon is visited by the Queen of Sheba.

A nineteenth-century view

For many years, people continued to tell and be amazed by these romantic tales of a ruined city full of gold which may have gone to fill the treasure chests of Biblical rulers. The first Western traveller to come across the ruins of Great Zimbabwe was an American called Adam Render. In 1871, he showed the German explorer Karl Mauch where the ruins lay. Mauch was very excited by the sight of the great walls, and he spent much of the next year measuring, sketching and making notes about the ruins. Mauch was sure that the old stories were true, and that in fact there were even closer links between the ruins and King Solomon and the Queen of Sheba. He said that Great Zimbabwe was a copy of the palace where the Queen of Sheba stayed when she visited Solomon in Jerusalem. This was the first of many strange theories about Great Zimbabwe that people thought up during the nineteenth century.

Adam Render shows the ruins of Great Zimbabwe to Karl Mauch.

The Great Enclosure is surrounded by a stone wall over 10 metres high.

The ruins of Great Zimbabwe

Great Zimbabwe is actually two main groups of ruins. The first is perched on a hilltop and is known as the Hill Fortress. The builders of the Hill Fortress used huge natural boulders in the walls, piling up smaller stones around and between them. The Hill Fortress has a commanding view over the countryside all around.

The second group of ruins is in the valley below the Hill Fortress. The biggest of these ruins is a huge oval-shaped area called the Great Enclosure. Around the Great Enclosure there is a stone wall 253 metres long and over 10 metres high in places. This huge wall was built from specially cut stones, with no mortar to hold them together. Inside the Great Enclosure, the most noticeable structure is a tower 9 metres high, without any doors, windows or stairs. What was it used for? People have had all sorts of ingenious ideas, but it's unlikely that we'll ever know the true answer to this question.

Excavations at Great Zimbabwe

The stories about Great Zimbabwe caused great excitement in Europe, particularly when they suggested that it was once the centre for the gold trade in eastern Africa. Unfortunately, this meant that the first excavators of Great Zimbabwe were interested only in looking for gold and other precious objects. They did not try to learn more about the history of the buildings themselves. Many parts of the ruins were damaged by gold hunters, and when gold artefacts were found they were melted down so that the metal could be re-used.

The first proper excavations at Great Zimbabwe were made by a British archaeologist, David Randall-MacIver, in 1905. He decided that the buildings were built by the local African people in the Middle Ages. If he was right, all the stories about King Solomon and the Queen of Sheba were just that – stories. His report stirred up a great deal of argument. Many people didn't want to believe his evidence, but it was backed up by another archaeologist, Gertrude Caton-Thompson, in the early 1930s.

ZIMBABWE'S NATIONAL EMBLEM

The excavators at the ruins of Great Zimbabwe dug up several sculptures of birds, made out of a kind of soft stone called soapstone. One of these birds was perched on the top of a pole, with a crocodile crawling up towards it. This bird has become the national emblem of the country of Zimbabwe.

The latest techniques for working out the age of materials have shown that Great Zimbabwe was built between AD 1100 and 1450. It was probably used as a trading centre for precious metals and possibly for slaves. This is less romantic, perhaps, than the stories that were once told about it. But many mysteries still remain, and Great Zimbabwe will always be a very impressive 'lost city'.

The mysterious tower inside the Great Enclosure at Great Zimbabwe. It has no doors, windows or stairs.

GHOST TOWNS

In January 1848, James Marshall and John Sutter discovered gold in the Sierra Nevada hills of California in the USA. Within six months, most of the people of California had left their homes and farms and rushed to the Sierra Nevada. The following year, people came from all over the world to try their luck in the goldfields. By the end of 1849, the population of California had shot up from 26,000 to over 115,000, and the biggest gold rush in history had begun.

A BIT OF LUCK

All that the goldhunters needed to bring with them was a shovel, a shallow pan or bowl, and a bit of luck! The gold lay on the beds of streams and rivers, and looking for it was simple. The gold hunters shovelled gravel from the river bed into their pan with some water. They then swirled the pan around until the light sand and gravel washed over the edge, leaving the heavier gold in the bottom of the pan.

The miners set up small camps in the valleys and gorges of the Sierra Nevada. They often gave their camps colourful names, such as Poverty Bar, You Bet, Red Dog and Rough and Ready. As more people came to California in the hope of 'getting rich quick', many of these camps grew into small towns, complete with hotels, restaurants, dance halls, saloon bars and shops.

Pioneer towns

Many of the miners who came to California were men who had left their wives and children at home. They planned to go back home once they had made their fortunes. They moved on when the gold seemed to run out, or when they heard that gold had been found somewhere else. Nearly everyone who travelled to California had only one idea – to make money quickly.

For this reason, the buildings in the mining towns were not really made to last. One miner described how the mining towns were built: '. . . of all kinds of possible materials, shapes and sizes, and in any spot,

Mining camps in the Californian hills quickly grew up into small towns.

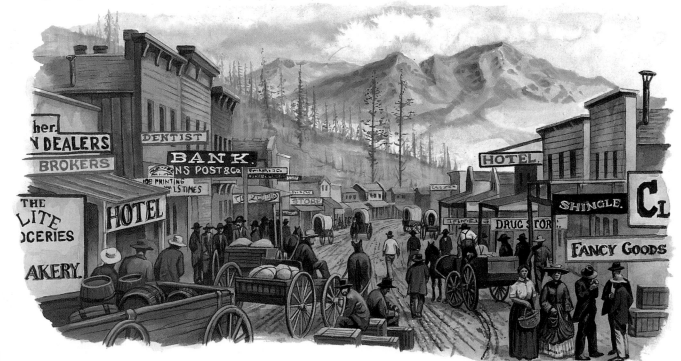

no matter how inconvenient, where the first storekeeper chose to pitch himself . . .'. The layout of the towns wasn't planned, and people used whatever materials were cheap and easy to find. Many buildings had wooden fronts, but the backs were made from timber frames with canvas roofs and walls – not much better than tents! Fire was always a danger, and some mining towns burned down and were rebuilt many times over.

Abandoned towns

One of the most famous gold rush towns, in the high desert land east of the Sierra Nevada, was called Virginia City. In 1859, gold and silver were found buried in the rock underground, and miners came rushing to dig it up. Soon, a bustling city grew up out of nothing. The novelist Mark Twain worked as a journalist in Virginia City for some time. He described a city full of people, with a police force, firefighters, shops, breweries, jails, theatres, banks, hotels, saloons and offices of all kinds. There were also large mills where the gold and silver were separated from the ore (rock) which held them.

Virginia City, Nevada, USA, as it looks today

In 1875, Virginia City had over 20,000 inhabitants. But in the 1880s the gold and silver began to run out, and the miners left in their thousands, lured by the rich promise of gold elsewhere. Virginia City was deserted almost as quickly as it had grown up. Today it is one of the hundreds of 'ghost towns' scattered all over the American West. All its buildings are still standing, as if the people had left only yesterday.

Bodie, California, is a true ghost town. In 1880, Bodie had a population of about 10,000. Today, it stands deserted in the high desert country to the east of the Sierra Nevada hills.

ROUGHING IT

Mark Twain described life in Virginia City in his book Roughing It. *The vein of precious metal running through the rock underground was called the Comstock Lode. Virginia City was built over part of the Comstock Lode, so there were mine tunnels directly beneath the streets and buildings of the city. This is how Mark Twain described the city in its heyday: 'It claimed a population of 15,000 to 18,000, and all day long half of this little army swarmed the streets like bees and the other half swarmed among the drifts and tunnels of the "Comstock", hundreds of feet down in the earth directly under those same streets. Often we felt our chairs jar, and heard the faint boom of a blast down in the bowels of the earth under the office.'*

UNSOLVED MYSTERIES

Today, excavating lost towns and cities is the work of highly trained teams of archaeologists. The days of amateur treasure hunters searching ruins for gold and other valuable objects are gone. But amazing finds are being made and new sites are still being uncovered, which all add to our knowledge of the past. Often, a new discovery forces archaeologists and historians to change their ideas about the past. Sometimes something so strange and unusual is found that it creates a whole new mystery . . .

A THEORY DISPROVED

When a Greek archaeologist, Spyridon Marinatos, began excavations on the island of Thera (Santorini) in 1967, he was hoping to find out the truth about the end of the Minoan civilization (see page 20). The Minoans lived on Crete, about 100 kilometres south of Thera, until around 1500 BC, when some sort of disaster brought their civilization to an end. Professor Marinatos thought that the cause may have been a huge volcanic eruption on Thera, which sent out clouds of dust and ash and set off huge tidal waves.

Professor Marinatos decided to excavate on Thera itself to find out more about the eruption. He dug deep trenches around the village of Akrotiri in the south of the island. Here he found houses preserved under the ash, just as at Pompeii (see page 22), but he found no human skeletons. It seems that the people had time to escape before the worst of the eruption. By working out the age of pieces of pottery and other remains, Professor Marinatos decided that Akrotiri was abandoned some years before the destruction of Knossos on Crete. This means that the eruption happened before the end of the Minoan civilization. So the destruction of Knossos is still a mystery, which may perhaps be solved in the future.

Ancient temple walls on the island of Thera

Minoan pottery found in Knossos, Crete

The 'Coppergate helmet', one of the many Viking artefacts discovered during the excavations of Jorvik in York, northern England.

HISTORY BENEATH THE SURFACE

In many modern-day towns and cities, history lies not very far beneath the surface! Many towns and cities are built on sites that have been inhabited for centuries. Obviously, archaeologists can't excavate easily where there are modern shops, offices or houses. But if a building is pulled down to make space for redevelopment, it is sometimes possible for the archaeologists to excavate the site first.

This is what has been happening in the city of York, in Britain. Archaeologists have gradually uncovered a Viking city, called Jorvik, beneath the modern city. Underneath the city centre, they have discovered the business centre of Jorvik, where craftspeople such as jewellers and woodworkers made and sold their goods. From their finds, they have been able to work out what life in the Viking city was like.

LEGENDARY CITIES

There are some 'lost' cities that will probably never be found. These are the cities that are described in legends, folktales and myths. The descriptions may once have been based on real places, but nowadays we do not know where the cities were, or even whether they ever really existed. Camelot, the legendary court and capital of King Arthur, is one of these places. Many people think that Cadbury Castle in Somerset, Britain, is the site of Camelot. Others say that the tale of King Arthur is just a story, and that Camelot was not a real place.

The strange tale of Atlantis is a mixture of history and legend. The Greek philosopher Plato (427–347 BC) wrote about the mysterious story of Atlantis, which is not a lost city but a whole lost island! The island is supposed to have disappeared under the waves after a volcanic eruption. Many people have tried to prove that the tale of Atlantis is actually the story of the end of the Minoan civilization. Others have suggested that Atlantis lies deep below the waves of the Atlantic Ocean. It is just one of the many mysteries of ancient times that will perhaps never be solved.

TENOCHTITLAN AND MEXICO

One morning in 1978, some workers were digging a ditch for new electrical cables in Mexico City, Mexico. As they dug through the damp earth, they came across the edge of a large stone. The stone was decorated with sculptures, and it was huge! Work stopped, and archaeologists came to investigate. What the workers had found was part of a temple from the Aztec city of Tenochtitlán, the capital of the Aztec Empire. Tenochtitlán was reduced to ruins within a few years of the Spanish invasion (see page 30), and Mexico City was built on its site. Archaeologists thought this find was so important that an office block was torn down so that they could investigate! The Aztec Great Temple, which had been hidden for 400 years, was uncovered.

GLOSSARY

archaeologist someone who makes a scientific study of the past, often by digging up buried objects and examining them closely

archaeology the study of human history from remains such as the sites of ancient cities and burial places

Assyrians people of the ancient empire that covered much of northern Mesopotamia. The Assyrian Empire reached its greatest extent between 700 and 650 BC

Aztecs the Aztecs ruled a great empire in Central America in the fifteenth and sixteenth centuries, until the arrival of the Spanish invader Cortés in 1519

baray a waterway built by the people of the Khmer Empire. In Angkor, many of these waterways were used for irrigation

Comstock Lode the rich vein of gold and silver found east of the Sierra Nevada mountains, California, USA, in 1859

conquistadors the Spanish conquerors who invaded Central and South America in the sixteenth century

cuneiform the name given by scholars to the wedge-shaped writing used by the early peoples of Mesopotamia

excavate to excavate something is to dig it up

Incas the Inca people ruled a huge empire in South America for about 100 years, until the invasion of the Spanish in 1532

Maya the people of Central America. Their civilization was destroyed by the arrival of the Spanish in the sixteenth century

Mesopotamia the ancient name for the land between the Tigris and Euphrates rivers in present-day Iraq

Minoans the people of an ancient civilization that flourished on the island of Crete from about 3000 to 1500 BC

missionary a member of a religious faith who tries to convert people to his or her faith

neo-classical a type of art in late eighteenth- and early nineteenth-century Europe that was inspired by the arts of Ancient Greece and Rome

ore rock that contains precious metal

quipu a length of knotted cord used by the Incas to keep records

Sumerians people of an ancient civilization based in southern Mesopotamia

ziggurat a kind of stepped temple built by the ancient peoples of Mesopotamia

INDEX

VIRGINIA
CITY

TENOCHTITLAN

MAYA CITIES
PALENQUE
COPAN

EL CEREN

INCA CITIES
MACHU PICCHU
CUZCO